Gay and Okay

Gay and Okay

A CONSERVATIVE CHRISTIAN'S
MIND CHANGE

John W Brown

Rev. date: 06/12/2014

To order additional copies of this book, contact:
Xlibris LLC
1-888-795-4274
www.Xlibris.com
Orders@Xlibris.com
603410

Contents

For Your Tears I Died

From deep within the tears I'm forced to cry
From deep within the pain I try to hide
They love to bash and call me trash,
But you, oh Lord, with arms open wide
Say, "For you I died."

And Jesus says, "Come to me—stand by my side,
I know you are hurting you won't be denied.
I love all my children—they are gold in my eyes
And always remember, 'For your tears I died.'"

Oh, why Lord would I want to choose this way?
When all it brings is hurt for just being gay?
But I know dear Lord, for me you chose this way.
So I thank you and praise you for how I am made
Use me Lord, in your own special way.

Your love so great I don't understand,
But I know you love all and on that I will stand
I know you're with me and always will be,
And thank you and praise you for all of my days
And I am going with you all of the way.

And Jesus says, "Come to me, stand by my side
I know you are hurting you won't be denied.
I love all my children—they are gold in my eyes
And always remember 'For your tears I died.'"

John W Brown

Preface

As a gay Christian, I have struggled for many years with the teachings of the Bible and homosexuality. I have tried to reconcile what I was taught, what I thought I understood the Bible to teach, and my own sexuality. This then is the story of my Christian journey and what I discovered. It is written so that others who may be struggling with the same misunderstandings can read it and relate. Hopefully through it you can come to find a loving God and acceptance and love for yourself and from others. It is also written for those who, although not gay, may be struggling with the concept. This may be because their church is debating whether or not to allow gays to be members of their church and be ordained to ministry. It may be because a member of their family is gay or they know someone who is gay. Perhaps they are just curious. Whatever the reason, I invite you to follow my journey of discovery with an open mind and heart.

This book is intended to be an open invitation to all to come, learn, understand, and know the truth. It is not meant to discredit any church; therefore I have avoided listing the names of any local churches to which I have belonged. It is intended as a tool for reconciliation, and the unifying of the whole body of Christ including gays, lesbians and trans-gender people. As Christian brothers and sisters, let us find the Biblical truth about homosexuality and what God thinks of it. Will you do that?

All scripture references are taken from the New King James Version of the Bible unless otherwise noted. All references to Hebrew or Greek meanings are taken from Strong's Exhaustive Concordance of the Bible English definitions are taken from the Random House College Dictionary. I need to thank my editors, Patricia Brush, a "cradle Anglican" who resides in Ottawa, Ontario, Canada. Her life-long interest in music, theology and clarity of language inspired her work. The design editor, Graham Warden, who has wide experience and a literary-science gift of language, now residing in the Australian capital, Canberra. Thanks also to Marlene Campbell, the Rev. Dr. John Mather Lurvey, the Disciplined Order of Christ and so many others. They have loved me, prayed with me, and helped me to realize and then accept who I am. Their support gave me the courage to write about my journey and share it with others. "Free at last, free at last, thank God almighty we're free at last" Dr. Martin Luther King, Jr.

Introduction

What does the Bible say about homosexuality? Does it condemn it as many of us have been led to believe? As a Christian pastor and Bible teacher for over forty years I have struggled with these two questions. Although raised in the Congregational faith, I later became a member of the Church of Christ denomination, then a Pentecostal, an Episcopalian, and finally a member of an Independent Catholic Church, which I still am today. I have known since I was twelve years old that I was different and gay. Coming from a very strict, evangelical, conservative background, homosexuality was not allowed. That was especially true for preachers. It was seen as the unpardonable sin, which could cause you to burn forever in hell; therefore, I remained firmly in the closet.

Believing homosexuality was wrong, I did the traditional things; dating women and becoming engaged to be married four times, but never going through with it. In my first church I was an associate pastor, and later fired upon suspicion that I might be gay. Through the succeeding years, I had two gay relationships which were ended when the church learned about them. I had hands laid on me to cast out the "demon of homosexuality" and even was turned over a pastor's knee to have the demon spanked out of me. I had a belt used on me to drive the demon out. I fasted and prayed for deliverance, and for God to change me; all to no avail. I even joined two different religious communities. I thought that if I could be in a place where people loved God, wanted to serve Him and their fellow man, pray and study the Word, this could be my path to freedom. That had mixed results.

I couldn't try anything within the community as that would have provoked an uproar and I would have been kicked out. However, none of these actions changed my desires. I had a friend from outside the community whom I would see periodically for sex. I even underwent counseling to try and convince me that I was not gay, but a normal "guy," whatever that means. My life was filled with guilt and condemnation for not being what I thought God wanted me to be. I questioned why God was not hearing my prayers and answering them. I was trying to be something I was not because I knew no other way to be. More than anything else, I wanted to serve God and love Him with everything I had. Yet, in this one area it seemed I was defeated over and over again. I believed that Satan had a stranglehold on me and was not about to let go, no matter what I did. Was Satan more powerful than God? It seemed that way. I had done everything my church said I needed to do to be free from this "sin", yet I hadn't succeeded. I was told instead that I was weak, immature, needed to love God more, and read the Word and memorize it. I was told that if I would just quote the Word to the devil—whenever tempted—pray more for "deliverance", have more faith, claim my deliverance and stand on it, I'd be free and Satan would flee. I was told to avoid all contact with gay people, including my brother who was gay, lest they "ensnare me into their lifestyle". That turned out to be a vicious merry-go-round of trying to do and be what everyone said I should be. I'd redouble my efforts to be free of my desires only to fail over and over again. There seemed to be no relief and no escape for me.

Finally, at a point of sheer desperation, I put down all the teachings I had on the subject of homosexuality, including any preconceived ideas I may have had. I began to let God speak to me and was led by God to do a study on the subject of homosexuality from a biblical perspective. I expected it to confirm my worst nightmares and fears. I felt sure it would leave me feeling even more confused and condemned. Instead, I was pleasantly surprised to find it very enlightening and not at all what I expected. For the first time I felt free and at peace. I found out God was not mad at me nor did God hate me for being gay. In fact, God had made me the way I am and He loved me. God wasn't condemning me, but wanted to receive me with open arms into His family. God also wanted to use me in ministry for His glory, despite what others might think of my being gay. The following is the result of that study. It is the beginning of a journey to freedom and the realization that I am gay and it is okay. All I ask, if you are gay, is that this might be a source of enlightenment for you. That it would be the road to full deliverance for you into all that God has for you as a gay person who loves God, wanting to serve and please Him. If you are not gay, please read this with an open mind, letting God speak to you concerning the things I will be sharing here.

My hope is that it will bring a better and fuller understanding of who gays are. The study will show you, I pray, what God really thinks of those of us who are gay and love God with all our hearts. Having said that, let's begin our journey through the pages of scripture and history and see what we can find out about homosexuality. This study will be from both a biblical perspective and a historical point of view, especially as it relates to traditional teaching and also apostolic teaching on homosexuality. We will see how it applies to us today. For those who are gay, I pray that by the time we're through you will be able to say "Free at last, free at last, thank God almighty we're free at last". May this be the liberation day for you into all you can be in Christ.

We should not reinterpret the Bible to fit our own biases and prejudices. We must have a church of integrity to maintain our moral authority as the church; however, we do need to examine the original biblical texts to find what they really say and cast off centuries of bias and prejudice that have been layered onto the text. For more than 1500 years Christians supported the slave trade by using statements from Paul and other biblical writers, but there has been a godly progressive move through history that has worked to bring more freedom, integrity, and worth to people. The progressive voice within the church was in the forefront of the battle to end slavery, and in the Civil Rights movement to win basic rights for Black people and the right to vote. Progressive church voices supported the battle for the separation of church and state, and the adoption of the amendment to the Constitution guaranteeing religious freedom to all. In many other issues, from better hospital care to free public education, to prison reform, to women's suffrage, the progressive voices in the church spoke and helped make a difference. She still needs to be there today confronting the issues of our time with Christian love. She needs to be seeking to right any injustice she may find, as the church has done throughout the centuries.

When the church acts to correct a tradition, she is following in the footsteps of Jesus who corrected earlier traditions in his Sermon on the Mount (Matthew 5:21-48). Many Christians now believe that the love ethic of Jesus is more important than the proscriptions in the Old Testament and specific church regulations within the letters of Paul and Peter in the New Testament. For example, Paul confronted various issues in the local churches. He addressed those issues peculiar to each church and set rules for them; however, they were for that local church only and not necessarily for the whole body of Christ. When we try to take a message for an ancient local church and apply it now to the global church, we can misinterpret the text. Learning how to apply Bible truths and Paul's teachings to the church today may require fresh efforts to grasp the principles within the biblical text. To do that, we need to seek and follow as the Holy Spirit reveals God's mind to us. Add to that, new scientific research and study concerning sexual orientation. We have access to much more information and understanding about homosexuality than our forebears knew. In light of new evidence, which increasingly shows same-sex orientation from birth, the church's progressive voice stands for a new biblical interpretation that challenges previous church condemnations.

Finally, I discovered three things, described later in fuller detail, that challenged traditional, Bible-based church opposition to homosexuality. First, as in the case of Sodom, you'll see the Bible text actually opposed heterosexual men sexually assaulting other men No problems with that. Neither does the Sodom case speak against a loving, consensual, same-sex relationship. This I believe Paul also assumed when he opposed same-sex relationships in Romans 1:18-25. He spoke against men engaged in sexual relations contrary to their nature (physis in Greek). Those whose nature is same-sex oriented, would not enter a same-sex relationship contrary to their nature. Paul's criticism applied to heterosexual or at most, bi-sexual men or women, sexually engaging other heterosexual men or women of their same gender. A similar point applies to Paul's "anti-gay" remark in 1 Corinthians 6:9-10. Second, Jesus recognized those who are born eunuchs in Matthew 19:12. He did not condemn them, but acknowledged their reality.

Recent historical scholarship shows a tolerance in ancient cultures, including the church in early centuries, and later among Byzantine Christians in the medieval period, for men called eunuchs. They were not always castrated or physically unable for sexual activity. They simply did not desire to assume the traditional male role of father and husband. Sometimes called, a third gender, these men rose to prominence in ancient Egypt, India, Persia, Greece, Roman and Byzantine societies and within the church. Scholars today identify some of these men as sharing the characteristics of those we call gay men today. I found this tolerance of born eunuchs included possibly same-sex unions within the church. Third, the strong anti-homosexual tradition in Western Christianity, at least in part, arose when Roman Emperor Theodosius made a decree against the Arian sect of Christians in 390 CE. He did so for political reasons to gain favor with powerful orthodox Christian bishops such as Ambrose of Milan. The Church in the West wanted to purge born eunuchs in church and political leadership, because they supported Arian theology. Since Arian Christians did not believe in the full divinity of Jesus, Orthodox Christian leaders opposed them. If the anti-gay tradition within the Western Christian Church rests upon political, rather than clear biblical foundations, then traditional Christians need to re-examine their views. For too long fear drove Christian gay people into the closet. It is time to embrace what the Bible, science and history tell us, what I believe God wills for us also, and free gay people to be what they were created to be.

The Bible

WHY DID GOD DESTROY SODOM
AND GOMORRAH?

As we begin this study, many of our evangelical Christian brothers and sisters, who love the Lord, would insist that the Bible condemns homosexuality unequivocally. They believe all homosexuals choose to be what they are and, in so doing, have turned their backs on God. They reject the idea that the majority of homosexuals are born that way. Other Christians, myself included, would say gays and lesbians (homosexuals) are made that way and it's not something they consciously chose. They believe that God loves them and accepts them as they are and that the Bible does not condemn them. So who is right?

One of the first texts most evangelicals will point to as a condemnation of homosexuality is found in Genesis in the19th chapter. They insist that the story is about God destroying the cities of Sodom and Gomorrah because of the inhabitants' homosexual behavior; however, is that what this story is really all about? Did God actually destroy the cities of Sodom and Gomorrah for the "sin" of homosexuality or is there another reason? First, we need to recognize that there is no specific mention of homosexuality in the Bible. Neither do the words homosexual or homosexuality appear in the Bible in the original languages in which it was written. The closest we can come to homosexuality is the word sodomite, which originally referred to a temple or male prostitute.

The first mention of Sodom (from which our word sodomite comes) is found in Genesis in the 19th chapter. As we look at this chapter, I want us to think about whether or not the men of Sodom were actually homosexuals. We will discover the Bible taught a different reason why God destroyed the people of Sodom and Gomorrah. Let us look at this passage as well as a correlating one in Ezekiel. We will find a different reason why God destroyed the two cities. Consider the Genesis account first and see what characteristics we find about the men of Sodom and the reasons why God destroyed them. In the Genesis 19 account, there are two characteristics that describe the men of Sodom.

A.   The Men of Sodom Were Rapists

As we begin to delve into this chapter, the first thing that stands out is that the men of Sodom were planning to rape the angels who were staying with Lot. This was not to be an act of love between two people of the same sex. It was instead to be a brutal rape of the angels. *Now before they lay down, the men of the city, the men of Sodom, both old and young, all the people from every quarter, surrounded the house. And they called to Lot and said to him, Where are the men who came to you tonight? Bring them out to us that we may know them carnally. [1].*

One of the definitions for rape is "any act of sexual intercourse forced upon another". This is what the men of Sodom intended to do to the angels if the angels had not struck them blind. They mistakenly thought the angels were humans who had received hospitality at Lot's house. The men of Sodom wanted Lot to surrender the angels so that they could rape them. Not a loving act, but one which would have left the angels degraded, humiliated, and violated.

In ancient times when men were captured in battle or discovered to be spies, the victors would rape them. This was to prove their superiority over them as well as to degrade and belittle the losers by making them assume the submissive, female role in sex. It was assumed that no self-respecting male would do thus. The loservictims would be stripped of their masculinity, made to feel inferior and to begin to accept their new role as slaves. This could be what the men of Sodom had in mind. The Bible always condemns rape. Sex should be a loving act between two people, not one that is forced upon another without their consent. In this case the men of Sodom were not asking the angels whether or not they wanted to have sex. Instead, they were to be forcibly raped.

B. Heterosexual Men of Sodom Participated

The biblical record says that these were all the men both young and old of Sodom. These were, for the most part, heterosexual men. *Please my brethren, do not so wickedly! See now, I have two daughters who have not known a man; please let me bring them out to you, and you may do to them as you wish; only do nothing to these men, since this is the reason they have come under the shadow of my roof. [2].*

Laying aside the moral question of a father giving his virgin daughters to be raped by violent men, let us consider this question: Why did Lot offer his daughters to these men unless he was sure that they were heterosexual and would accept his offer? That is, Lot assumed the men of Sodom would take his daughters, rape them and leave the angels unmolested. *So Lot went out and spoke to his sons-in-law, who had married his daughters, and said, "Get up, get out of this place; for the Lord will destroy this city." But to his sons-in-law he seemed to be joking. [3].*

Lot and his sons-in-law were not the only married men in Sodom. Being married appeared then as common as it has been in every society. While marriage does not necessarily preclude homosexuality, the vast majority of these men would more probably be classified today as heterosexual. In summation, if the men of Sodom had not been stopped by the angels, this would have been a violent rape perpetrated by heterosexual men on the angels, who they thought were men.

There is also something else that needs to be mentioned here. The word for men used here is a generic term and can be translated as human kind also. This raises then the possibility there were women in the crowd that night. This would agree with the passage we looked at earlier where it says all the people came. Perhaps it was to cheer their husbands on as they dominated the angel-men and showed their superiority. (Were some of the women hoping to have sex with the angels?) In any case, the crowd was not made up of exclusively homosexual men. Instead, these were crazed men ready to do anything to get what they wanted.

C. Homosexuality was not Sodom's abomination

To get an even better idea of why God chose to destroy Sodom and Gomorrah we need to look at a correlating passage in Ezekiel. There we find six reasons why God destroyed Sodom and Gomorrah. *Look, this was the iniquity of your sister Sodom; She and her daughter had pride, fullness of food, and abundance of idleness; neither did she strengthen the hand of the poor and needy. And they were haughty and committed abomination before Me; therefore I took them away as I saw fit. [4].*

What was their abomination? As used here in the Hebrew, abomination means something disgusting, abhorrent, and idolatrous in a custom or thing. We can understand it better by looking at the word iniquity. It means evil, fault, moral perversity, mischief, and sin. God shows us exactly what He considers sin and abomination by listing six things in this passage.

1.   They had pride

As used in this passage, pride means to be arrogant, and pompous. My dictionary defines arrogant as: a. Making unwarrantable claims or pretensions to superior importance or rights. b. A feeling of superiority or an offensive exhibition of it. c. Presumptuous or overbearing conduct and statements resulting from such conduct.

This shows us that the people of Sodom felt themselves to be superior to others, making the others feel inferior by their words and actions. My dictionary defines pompous as: a. Characterized by an ostentatious display of dignity or importance. b. Ostentatiously lofty or high flown c. Characterized by pomp, stately splendor or magnificence.

It also defines ostentatious as being a pretentious display, with the act of showing or exhibiting manners or actions intended to attract notice. Thus the men of Sodom believed they were superior to everyone else. This led them to act accordingly in a way which would attract attention to this superiority and their feeling of self-importance. In other words, they were not humble but full of self-importance, and a disdain for anyone or anything not matching up to their standard. That however, was just the beginning.

2.   They had fullness of food

As used here, fullness of food means to be in a state of satisfaction with one's appetite or desire to the point of boredom. Did you catch that they had so much stuff they were bored with it? Maybe boredom led them to Lot's door that night seeking a new high or thrill. This was probably reinforced by the next reason God gives for their destruction.

3. They had an abundance of idleness
This refers to having everything that they needed as well as peace, prosperity and quietness, so much so that they did not need to work to maintain their situation. This could appear to be a good thing, but there was a problem with that picture, from God's perspective, as we see in the next charge He brings against them.

4. They failed to strengthen the hands of the poor and needy
The men of Sodom refused to help the poor and needy. This was not because they did not have it to give. They had it, but chose to hoard it to themselves rather than give it away. In the twenty-fifth chapter of Matthew, Jesus teaches a parable concerning sheep and goats. According to Jesus, a sheep is concerned about others and uses what he has to help others. Wherever he sees a need, whether it is a hungry or thirsty person, one who is naked or homeless or in prison, he wants to help them. Goats, like the men of Sodom, refuse to do that; hoarding everything to themselves. Sheep will be rewarded and goats will be punished at the judgment seat of Christ.

5. They were haughty
As Ezekiel used it here, it means to soar, to be lifted up, to be proud, and to be raised up to a great height. Due to the fact that they believed they were superior, they acted accordingly. They refused to help those they considered to be inferior to them. As a consequence, they became inflated with pride, raising themselves up to great heights above others. This was a certain recipe for disaster as they were committing the very act that caused Lucifer-Satan's expulsion from heaven. *How you have fallen from heaven, O Lucifer, son of the morning! How you are cut down to the ground, you who weaken the nations! For you have said in your heart: "I will ascend into heaven, I will exalt my throne above the stars of God; I will also sit on the mount of the congregation on the farthest sides of the north; I will ascend above the heights of the clouds I will be like the most High." Yet you shall be brought down to Sheol, to the lowest depths of the Pit.* [5].

Five times Satan exalted himself, boasting of what he is going to do. God, however, has other ideas. Instead, God casts him down from heaven to Sheol or the grave. The people of Sodom and Gomorrah felt that they were better than anyone else; therefore they felt they could do whatever they wanted and were accountable to no one. They were about to find out differently as they were cast down also. They also didn't realize or care that God opposed pride and arrogance among other things. King Solomon writes: *Pride goes before destruction and a haughty spirit before a fall. [6].*

As we have seen, the people of Sodom and Gomorrah were full of pride and haughtiness, which would make them ripe for destruction and a big fall. By doing the previous five things, God said it led them to commit a sixth thing.

6.   The Root Abomination: Sodom's Refusal of Hospitality to Strangers I defined abomination earlier as something disgusting, abhorrent, and idolatrous in a custom or thing. The five listed faults add up to the sin of inhospitality which is the abomination. None of these faults have anything to do with homosexuality. According to the ancient teaching of Jewish rabbis, the people of Sodom and Gomorrah didn't like strangers and did everything they could to discourage them from coming into their land. If they did come then they wanted to make sure no food or drink was consumed by them and no shelter was offered them. The penalty for helping a stranger in anyway was death. This in spite of the fact they had so much food they were bored with it. That means they had enough to feed strangers but instead chose to hoard it to themselves. They even stretched nets over the trees to keep the birds from eating of the fruit of the trees. The rabbis also taught that Lot had had an older daughter who was caught helping a stranger and taken out and stoned to death. Lot knew what had happened to his daughter, and therefore of the law against helping strangers; however, he chose to deliberately disobey the law and take the strangers into his home. He also chose to feed them and offer them shelter for the night. The men of Sodom could have been vigilantes coming to enforce the law and stone Lot for taking in and feeding a stranger, and to stone the strangers for daring to eat the food of Sodom and accept the hospitality of someone living there.

One other possibility here is that the men of Sodom thought the angels might be spies. If so they then wanted to check them out, finding out their intentions for traveling to Sodom. This is a real possibility when we consider that a short time earlier the city had been attacked, defeated and everyone, along with everything they owned was carried off into captivity. They were only saved by the intervention of Abram and his coming and rescuing them. If that be the case, then this would have been a very serious matter and Lot's refusal to hand them over for interrogation would invite suspicion and harsh treatment.

Summing up, we have seen that Sodom and Gomorrah were full of pride, haughtiness, and refusal to look after those in need; sins God opposed. Any of these sins would have been cause for Him to destroy them. This shows much about the character of God. He cares about injustice, and anything that is not birthed and brought forth in love. It shows that He will deal with these wrongs accordingly. Far from being a treatise on homosexual behavior, the story of Sodom and Gomorrah is a warning against arrogance, haughtiness, hoarding while ignoring the needs of those around us, and treating others with contempt. These are the issues which led to the destruction of Sodom and Gomorrah. The decision to destroy Sodom and Gomorrah was made before the attempted rape of the angels.

The story is not about homosexuality and the love between two people of the same sex. Ezekiel and the ancient rabbis teach what they believe to be the real story of Sodom. It is about choice. Lot made a bad choice when he moved to Sodom. He let the place so influence his thinking that he and his family were reluctant to leave and had to be forcibly evicted from Sodom in order to save their lives. Even then, Lot's wife disobeyed and looked back, turning into a pillar of salt. Lot lost everything except for the clothes on his back; a heavy price to pay for making a wrong decision. Later he would get drunk and commit incest with both his daughters, having children by them. Like Lot, the decisions we make can affect us and others for a long time. They can also affect the way we perceive and act.

This leads to something about Lot we need to consider. In 2 Peter 2:7, it says that Lot was a righteous man who was tormented by what he saw in Sodom. In the Greek it means that he was vexed, labored down, and oppressed by what he saw. Obviously he wasn't bothered enough to move out; however, could he have been bothered enough to preach a message condemning them and their lifestyle?

In Genesis 19:9, one of the charges the men of Sodom make against Lot is that he keeps on judging them. Could that be why they rejected Lot's message when he tried to warn of the coming destruction of the city? In Genesis 19:14, it says Lot's sons-in-law thought he was joking. Could they have been thinking "Oh yeah, right, Lot. You're always condemning us. We know you don't like or approve of us. You're just a fanatic and a bigot. Since we haven't listened to you before now, you are going to try to scare us into doing what you want. Not going to work preacher. Good night." Could it be he was just a thorn in their side at best, and a crank to be laughed at and ignored? Are we like Lot, today? There is a saying, "So heavenly-minded that they're no earthly good." Many want to preach and tell everyone how they should live, but they themselves have problems walking the talk themselves. They forget the admonition of Jesus to remove the log from their eye first, and then they can see clearly to remove the speck from their brother's eye. Could that have been Lot's problem? He could see all the sins of his neighbors, but couldn't see the log in his own eye?

I believe it is worth consideration. The destruction of Sodom and Gomorrah had little to do with what we call homosexuality. Are there other passages in the Bible that condemn the practice? Perhaps, but don't count on it. We will look at other texts of scripture often cited to condemn homosexuality and see if they really do that. Meanwhile, I hope you received some food for thought. Are you questioning what you previously believed concerning Sodom and Gomorrah? Are you ready to learn and see things in a new and refreshing way? If so, move on with me to the next chapter.

Chapter 1

IS GAY SEX OK?

Some use two scriptures found in Leviticus to condemn homosexuals. *You shall not lie with a male as with a woman. It is an abomination. [7].*

If a man lie with a male as he lies with a woman, both of them have committed an abomination. They shall surely be put to death. [8].

On the surface, these scriptures seem to settle the issue that homosexual practice is an abomination and should result in death for the participants. Some would understand this as proof that sex should only take place between a man and woman. Does this interpretation settle the issue or do these verses mean something else? The two passages found in Leviticus 18:22 and 20:13, belong in two lists of unholy behaviors practiced by the native peoples of Canaan and Egypt (18:2-3, 20:23-24) Moses hears God calling the Israelite peoples to ethical practices different from native Canaanite culture. To institute these holy practices, Moses interpret's God's will to require death or capital punishment for violators of many of these bans (20:2-21). The capital offenses include child sacrifice to the god Molech (v. 2), "(I) f any turn to mediums and wizards"(v. 6), cursing parents,(v.9) and adulterers, both male and female (v. 10). Chapter 20 records a second list of capital offenses involving sexual intimacy. "Uncovering the nakedness of" expresses the biblical metaphor for sexual union.

The list of specific sexual capital offenses include sexual union with his father's wife (v. 11), a man with his daughter-in-law (v. 12), If a man lies with a male as with a woman (v. 13), a man takes a wife and her mother (v. 14), sexual relations between a man or woman and an animal require death of both person and animal (v. 15-16), sexual union with a sister or the daughter of a parent (v. 17), If a man lies with a woman having her sickness . . . her flow of blood (v. 18) and sexual union with your mother's or father's sister or uncle's or brother's wife. In these last two cases, the wife of an uncle or brother is viewed as property made impure by the sexual act. (v. 19-21). Those who practice any one of the offenses listed above should be killed, says Moses. Later, in the same list, Moses includes the division of clean and unclean animals.

He bans eating the flesh of unclean animals such as pork (v. 25). How do we interpret these lists for Christians and especially verses 18:22 and 20:13 that ban and punish by death, a man who lies with a male as with a woman? Is male-male sex like the still-current ban of child sacrifice for religious worship? Or is the ban of a man lying with a male as with a woman more like sexual union during menstruation or eating unclean animals such as pork, which we no longer consider perversion? Is the ban's scope limited to men who assume the bodily posture of passivity during same-sexual intimacy, like the traditional passive female submitting to the dominant male? Might a different more mutually giving posture during male-male coitus escape the ban?

Bible-based Christian's should consider further limitations upon this list of forbidden practices. First, because of the influence of Jesus' ethic of love and forgiveness, we find taking the life of people engaging in alternative religious practices or sexual misconduct too severe. Second, as stated above, we no longer consider some acts a major offense such as sexual congress during menstruation or eating the meat of an unclean animal. Third, many of the provisions of these laws limit themselves to male behavior. For example, female-female sexual union is not forbidden in Lev. 20:13, only the male-male relations. One-sided bans seem unfair and weaken the credibility of the ethical principle it expresses. Fourth, again under the influence of Jesus' ethic of love and forgiveness, we no longer hold wives to be property of husbands. We no longer execute persons for violating property rights. Fifth, the holiness code of the Hebrew Bible, that includes these bans, became the basis for acts of religiously sanctioned genocide by the Israelites against the native peoples of Canaan/Palestine in Joshua chapters six through 11 and elsewhere. Christian ethics now reject such violent acts against the "unholy" in both ancient and the more recent Nazi acts of genocide against Jews, Stalin's genocidal policy against the kulaks and various groups in the old Soviet Union, Mao and the Gang of Six's mass killings in the People's Republic of China and the mass killings in Cambodia (Asia), Sudan, Nigeria, Somalia and Rwanda in modern Africa. Put in a positive way, Christian sexual ethics draw upon timeless biblical principles consistent with Jesus' ethics of love and forgiveness. Christian ethics require boundaries against irresponsible and destructive sexual behavior that destroy families and break the marriage covenant. Yet today, Jesus' ethics of love and forgiveness, summon the faithful to live by more than simple lists of forbidden or "unholy" practices. For these reasons, I don't believe the bans in 18:22 and 22:13 apply to a mutual, committed, loving relationship between people of the same sex.

That being the case, I believe it is time to challenge and lay aside these Old Testament prohibitions against homosexuality. We do so for another good reason. As New Testament Christians we are no longer under the laws of the Old Testament, as Paul argued in his Letter to the Galatians, where he opposed those claiming salvation by doing the works of keeping the Old Testament laws. Instead, Paul argued for freedom and liberty in the Holy Spirit. He realized that no one could be saved by keeping the law; salvation only comes by faith in Jesus Christ. It is time to allow gay people to be a full part of the Christian community, included in all aspects of church life as well as ministry.

The Apostle John sums it up this way: *And this is His commandment that we should believe on the name of His Son Jesus Christ, and love one another, as He gave us commandment. [9].*

We did the first part of the commandment, the believing, when we made a conscious decision to follow Christ and His teachings. The second part is to love one another. Please note that John does not give us any exceptions. He does not say love all but those you do not like, those who are different from you, or those who are gay, lesbian, bisexual or transgender. He says love one another. Period. Are we ready to allow gay, lesbian and transgender people to be a full part of the Christian community, included in all aspects of church life as well as ministry? Some may think that surely the New Testament is different. Surely, Jesus and the apostles condemn homosexuality. Are you sure? If you dare, follow me, and let's see what the New Testament has to say about homosexuality.

Chapter 2

WHAT DOES JESUS HAVE TO SAY
ABOUT HOMOSEXUALITY?

It may surprise some to note that Jesus was practically silent on the subject of homosexuality. The few times that he speaks on the subject of sex and marriage, Jesus is more concerned with polygamy and fornication than anything else. This would explain why He makes the rule of one man, one wife for His church. Does that prohibit loving relations between two people of the same sex? Fornication, as used by Jesus in the Beatitudes, refers to three things: adultery, incest, and harlotry. Jesus says nothing about a loving relationship between two people of the same sex. An argument cannot be made that this is a prohibition against homosexuality.

The actions of Jesus speak louder than words. In the eighth chapter of Matthew, a centurion comes to Jesus looking for healing for his servant. At that time, a male servant was kept by a dominant man for sex when his wife or other women weren't around. He would take the male servant to have sex with him, especially before a battle. So it is a possibility that the servant was a sex slave of the centurion. If that is the case, Jesus healed a sex slave. There are no words of judgment or condemnation of the relationship between the master and his slave. Instead, Jesus honors the centurion as a great man of faith like no one else He had ever met. This then raises the question: Did Jesus know of their relationship and heal the servant anyway? If so, would that mean that Jesus looked at same-sex intimacy differently than do many Christians today?

Academic historians and scholars in Gender Studies analyzed evidence showing ancient and medieval cultures gave a high status to eunuchs. Medieval historian Kathryn M. Ringrose's scholarly study of eunuchs in Byzantine Christian culture from 600 to 1100 CE (also known as AD) concluded eunuchs formed a special social group that enjoyed high levels of trust and occupied positions of power.[10].

Indeed they formed a third category beyond traditional male and female roles. Gender Studies scholars such as Mathew Kuefler reason that "born eunuchs" or non-castrated men who played the role of eunuch included gay men who did not follow the traditional male role in society of procreator of a family. [11].

Mattai the Preacher a gay Christian intellectual with a degree from University of California-Berkeley and an evangelical Christian background, pushed the eunuch gay man connection back in history to include ancient Egypt, Babylon and Persia. His website homosexual eunuchs in the bible.com discloses the point of view he advocates.[12].

For example, Mattai uses word studies of ancient languages such as Hebrew and Aramaic to show evidence that the biblical figure Daniel may have been a born eunuch/gay man rather a castrated one. Mattai cites biblical passages in Daniel 1:4, 1:9 and 14:2 that report the affection of the chief eunuch and king for Daniel. Mattai argues this shows evidence of a gay sexual attraction. Mattai and others then argue that Jesus' statement in Matthew 19:12 refers to gay men who were "born eunuch." *For there are eunuchs who were born thus from their mother's womb, and there are eunuchs who were made eunuchs by men, and there are eunuchs who have made themselves eunuchs for the kingdom of heaven's sake . . . [13].*

Jesus' statement reflects a three part division of the social group described as eunuchs. They are as follows:
1. Born eunuchs
2. Castrated eunuchs
3. Those that have chosen to make themselves eunuchs for the kingdom of heaven.

If that is the case, would that mean that Jesus did not make critical remarks about the first group that may have included gay men? Although there may not be a definitive answer one way or the other, I believe it merits some thought and prayer. Since they couldn't, or wouldn't procreate with women, eunuchs would not have been considered fully male. Using that definition of eunuch as a third category neither male, nor female, the critical biblical comments elsewhere might be speaking of a heterosexual male having sex with another heterosexual male. Some gay Christians like myself, would agree that such is forbidden and an abomination. (This offers further evidence that Paul's apparent anti-gay comment Romans 1, cited above, may not be directed at born eunuchs/gay men, but at hetero-sexual men engaging in forced sex or rape.)

Further, eunuch's could own property, vote, leave an inheritance and marry. However, castrated men were not allowed to do any of these things. More will be said about the role of born eunuchs/gay men in early church leadership and their banishment by Emperor Theodosius's decree against Arians in the year 390 CE in chapter six. This line of historical reconstruction suggests that gay men enjoyed status in early Christianity as they played out the role of social eunuch. Is there evidence of acceptance of this type of gay man in ministry and even same-sex unions in the early church? It is my conviction based upon this evidence that Jesus accepted born eunuchs/gay men without condemnation. Note further evidence of eunuch/gay men in church leadership. The first convert from Ethiopia, and the apostle to that land, was an eunuch. He served as the head of the treasury for Queen Candace and was returning from Jerusalem when Philip met him. Philip led him to salvation, baptized him, and then sent him on his way. The eunuch returned to Ethiopia where he helped establish the Christian Church. This would mean that one of the first converts to Christianity, and the person who established the Christian Church in Ethiopia, was possibly a homosexual. [14].

Perhaps another idea of what Jesus thinks about homosexuals can be found in the last words He spoke prior to His ascension into heaven. This is what is called the "Great Commission". If you would listen to some of our evangelical brothers and sisters, you might think Jesus said to go preach the gospel to everyone but gay people. That is not what Jesus said. *Go into all the world and preach the gospel to every creature. [15].*

The word creature can be translated as person or people. *Go therefore and make disciples of all the nations, baptizing them in the name of the Father, and of the Son, and of the Holy Spirit . . . [16].*

Note that no one is excluded from hearing and receiving the Gospel. "All" and "every" are inclusive words that leave no one out; therefore, Jesus is inclusive in receiving all who come to Him, without exception. A disciple is a follower of someone. Since Jesus' message is inclusive, then all people can be his disciples including all gays, lesbians, bisexuals, transgenders, transsexuals and any other kind of person that there may be. Since Jesus is all inclusive, so will His true people be today. Some might ask: What about the apostles and apostolic teaching? Don't they condemn homosexuality? Maybe, but wait and see. In the next two chapters we will look at what the apostles taught about homosexuality. We will also look at what they taught from an historical standpoint and see where the anti-homosexual teaching comes from.

Chapter 3

WHAT DID THE APOSTLES TEACH
ABOUT HOMOSEXUALITY?

Did Paul condemn all homosexuals in Romans 1:21-28? Most of what is normally construed to be antigay/ homosexual verses come from the writings of the Apostle Paul. But was Paul really anti-gay? Could it be that his words have been misconstrued and misinterpreted? Could they have been twisted to say something that the apostle never intended for them to say? I believe the answer is yes. The first reading many evangelical and conservative Christians offer as proof of Paul being anti-gay is the Letter to the Romans. It would seem to be that way at first glance. After all, Paul speaks of men lying with men and women doing the same. He says they have left their natural instincts to lust after each other. So that is it. Paul hates gays and we are all going to hell. Whoa! Be careful how you read the chapter lest you miss completely what Paul is really talking about here. First, Paul is speaking of back-slidden or lapsed Christians, who knew God at one time, but walked away. Or he may refer to persons who know God through nature, but have not yet heard Jesus' gospel of God's love . . . . *although they knew God, they did not glorify Him as God, nor were thankful, but became futile in their thoughts, and their foolish hearts were darkened. [17].*

What Did the Apostles Teach about Homosexuality?

We are not told why they walked away, just that they did. This then would not apply to the millions of gay, lesbian, bi-sexual and transgender persons who love God with everything they have. They try to please Him as much as they can. They are like any other Christian, going to church, praying, doing good works, and trying to live up to what God expects of them. A committed gay Christian would not fit Paul's description of those he condemned. *And even as they did not like to retain God in their knowledge, God gave them over to a debased mind, to do those things which are not fitting. [18].*

Again, these are people who have rejected God. People who have chosen to forget they ever knew Him; therefore God has handed them over to a debased mind. There is nothing here about people who love God and who also happen to love someone of the same sex as themselves. Another mark of the people whom Paul condemns is that they are idol worshippers. *Professing themselves to be wise, they became fools, and changed the glory of the incorruptible God into an image made like corruptible man—and birds and four-footed animals and creeping things. Therefore God also gave them up to uncleanness, in the lusts of their hearts, to dishonor their bodies among themselves, who exchanged the truth of God for a lie, and worshiped and served the creature rather than the Creator who is blessed forever. [19].*

Many people worship things other than God including some gays; however, there are many gays who love God and His creation. They are perfectly well-balanced people. They are good Christians too. Another characteristic of the people Paul writes about is they are driven by lust. Lust is not love. They are total opposites. *For this reason God gave them up to vile passions. For even their women exchanged the natural use for what is against nature. Likewise also the men, leaving the natural use of the woman, burned in their lust for one another, men with men committing what is shameful, and receiving in themselves the penalty of their error which was due. [20].*

On the surface, it might seem that Paul is condemning homosexuality and gays. Is that really the case? Let's take a deeper look and see. The word Paul uses for natural is the Greek word physis. It is something that is done by natural instinct or is inborn. For those gays who were gay from birth, their sexual orientation is natural, and therefore not contrary to nature. We natural born gays did not choose to be what we are. It is how God made us; therefore it is our natural state. For natural homosexuals, it would be unnatural to have sex with someone of the opposite sex, just as it would be unnatural for a heterosexual person to have sex with someone who is the same sex as themselves. What Paul is saying here is for each to do what is natural to them. This is not a condemnation of natural born homosexuals or of being gay, as such. Paul writes against lust-driven people. Lust as defined in my Strong's Concordance of the Bible, means to have an excitement of the mind or a strong longing for something. A dictionary I read said it is a strong sexual craving or desire which is excessive, unrestrained, and overwhelming. The lustful person is selfish, not caring about anyone but themselves.

The New Testament ethic of love is the opposite of lust. My dictionary gives three definitions for love. They are as follows: a. An intense affectionate concern for another person. b. An intense sexual desire for another person. c. A strong fondness or enthusiasm for something or someone.

Real Christian love is an action verb that means more than intense sexual desire. It is about caring for someone other than oneself. It is about being concerned about the welfare of another and their well-being. It wants to share its life with another so together they can accomplish something good. If there is any hurt, pain, or need, love is there to do what it can to alleviate it or help fix the problem. If there is injustice, love will seek a way to correct it. I believe that Paul's words condemn lust; however, I don't believe the condemnation carries over into a loving and committed relationship between two people of opposite sex of or the same sex. Paul's critical words in Romans focused on people not guided by Christian love. Jesus said love is the identifying mark of His people; therefore I believe that Jesus would have no problem with a loving, affirming, committed relationship between two people. Neither do I believe did Paul. Instead, Paul used the ethic of love, based upon his understanding of the character of God. That divine character of love was also expressed in the famous saying in the First Letter of John 4:8, God is love. God, who by definition is the superior to all created beings, wants we creatures to love as well. We displease God when we don't. We displease God, as Paul said, when we put created beings or things higher in our worship, devotion and love that God's character of love.

Did Paul condemn all homosexuals in 1 Corinthians 6:9-10? Conservative Christians cite I Corinthians, the Apostle Paul has another comment on the subject.

There he says:

Do you not know that the unrighteous will not inherit the kingdom of God? Neither fornicators, nor idolaters, nor adulterers, nor homosexuals, nor sodomites, nor thieves, nor covetous, nor drunkards, nor revilers, nor extortionist will inherit the kingdom of God. [21].

There are a few things we need to see in these verses. [22].

The word "homosexual" is added and not found in the original Greek. Although the above is one possible translation of the Greek, the Greek is very imprecise as to its exact meaning.The word Paul uses here can mean effeminate, abuser of themselves with mankind, boy prostitutes, male prostitutes, pedophiles, sodomites, or maybe homosexuals, take your choice. It could include any of those or possibly all of them, again, take your choice. I have five different Bible translations in my home, none of which agrees as to the exact meaning of this verse. The words homosexual and homosexuality were unheard of until the 1800s when they were invented by modern thinkers to describe the attraction to someone of the same sex. They would have been added to the original Greek text by someone trying to interpret the passage to their own liking. Remember also, abusers of mankind cannot be in a loving relationship. Abuse is never about loving. It is the degrading, hurting, and humiliation of another person. It has no regard for the other person's wants, concerns, needs, or desires. It is about having unhealthy power over another person. I, too, believe this is wrong. Paul is writing about Greek society, where young men and slaves were forced into having sex. Because the dominant person was more powerful, or because of his position, or because he owned them, he could force them to serve him sexually. They would have no choice in the matter but to submit. Can we all agree that no one should ever be forced to have sex if they don't want it? Sex should be a loving act between two people who love and affirm each other and under those conditions only. It can be read that Paul had the intention of ending forced homoerotic relations. This should not place limits on same-sex relationships that are freely embraced, covenanted and guided by Christ. In these verses, the issue is the love versus lust argument again. I agree that lust is always condemned by the Bible as wrong. A covenant of fidelity changes that. For that is a covenant of love where each partner is loving and affirming of the other. It would be the same as the marriage vows in a traditional wedding ceremony. There each person pledges to love, honor and respect their partner in all circumstances until death parts them. I believe in that kind of relationship between gay people. A covenant of fidelity would also limit the possibility of promiscuity. Promiscuity is sinful as it is not based on love and concern for the other partner. Christ-centered unions are different. They put God first, are loving and affirming of each other, and truly seek what is best for the other from a platform of true love. We need to note too that Paul requires women to wear a covering on their head when in church, to be silent in a church, not to teach or be in authority over a man. These requirements have been abandoned in most of the modern church as having no relevance for us today. Perhaps it is time to go back and re-examine this perceived "ban" on homosexuality. The ban may have been for a specific time and a place but not necessarily for our time. I believe it is long overdue to remove the ban and the sooner we do the better.

Does Paul Condemn Homosexuality in 1 Timothy 1:10? The Apostle Paul also addresses the subject in I Timothy 1:10 when he is talking about the law. Among those for whom he says the law was made were sodomites. The King James version translates that as defile themselves with mankind. Exactly what does Paul mean here? The word Paul used here for defile means an abuser or sodomite. As I mentioned previously, sodomite refers to a temple or male prostitute. Abuse is not love, and prostitution is definitely forbidden throughout scripture by God. Gay love would not be meant here by Paul; therefore, this verse can't be used to condemn all forms of homosexuality. Does Paul Attack Homosexuality in 2 Timothy 3:3? Some might argue that Paul hits on the subject in 2 Timothy 3:3 when he says that in the last days men will be without natural affection. Going back to what I said earlier in my comment on Romans 1, a gay person's natural affection is to one of their own sex. It would be unnatural for them to be anything else. This verse is not a condemnation of all homosexuality.

Does Peter Condemn Homosexuality in 2 Peter 2:6 Some would want to use the words of the Apostle Peter against homosexuals. He writes: *And turning the cities of Sodom and Gomorrah into ashes condemned them to destruction, making then an example to those who afterward would live ungodly. [23].*

This only works against homosexuals if you believe that homosexuality is the reason God destroyed the cities of Sodom and Gomorrah. The biblical prophet Ezekiel believed that God destroyed them because of their lack of hospitality and their intention to rape. Therefore this verse doesn't apply. Does Jude Condemn Homosexuality? This concept is touched upon in Jude where he says: *As Sodom and Gomorrah, and the cities around them in a similar manner to these, having given themselves over to sexual immorality and gone after strange flesh, are set forth as an example, suffering the vengeance of eternal fire. [24].*

What sexual immorality did the men of Sodom and Gomorrah commit? As we have seen, it was the crime of rape and lust. It was not a loving act between two people of any sexuality, making it less likely that Jude had all gays in mind here. One other verse from Jude is sometimes used to condemn homosexuals. Jude 1:18-19 refers to people walking after their own ungodly lusts and who are sensual people. There are a couple of things to note here. First, these verses could only be applied to gays if you believe homosexuality is ungodly. A careful reading of the Bible proves otherwise. Secondly, it refers to these people having ungodly lusts and as being sensual. Let's break this down a bit. The word "ungodly" here refers to wickedness, "Lust", as used here, means a longing for something forbidden. "Sensual" refers to a person who is governed by his natural impulses, not by God. These verses cannot refer to millions of gay Christians who love God, are seeking to be controlled by Him, and live for His glory. Did John condemn all homosexual acts in Revelation? Some might say that the Apostle John addresses the issue in the Book of Revelation when he says: *But the cowardly, unbelieving, abominable, murderers, sexually immoral, sorcerers, idolaters, and all liars shall have their part in the lake which burns with fire and brimstone, which is the second death. [25].*

This is the verse our evangelical brethren use to condemn gays to burn forever. But is that what John is saying here? In the original Greek, the word translated as sexually immoral here is whoremonger. As used here a whoremonger can be a male prostitute, a debauchee, a libertine, or a fornicator. It does not refer to a loving relationship between two people of the same sex. Did Paul disqualify gay and lesbian persons from leadership in the Christian church in 1 Timothy 3:2? In his qualifications for bishops and deacons, the Apostle Paul reaffirms the requirement of Jesus that a leader in the church have one wife. Many scholars understand that this was a statement against the practice of polygamy. It does not automatically disqualify gays from either being

Christian or holding office in the church. They do need to be in a committed relationship or celibate. I believe the goal should always be for heterosexual and homosexual couples to live lives pleasing to God. If they are going to be in relationship with someone, the relationship should be committed and centered on Christ. The couple should be seeking God's will for their lives, and acting upon it. The Bible is teaching us that it is opposed to prostitution, and to anyone being forced into sexual services. It also supports the idea of marriage between one man and one woman in opposition to polygamy and to multiple marriages resulting from divorce and remarriage.

The Bible is either silent or ambivalent on the subject of homosexuality providing that relationships are loving, caring, and affirming. Perhaps we need to follow Jesus words when he says:

Judge not that you be not judged. For with what judgment you judge, you will be judged; and with the measure you use, it will be measured back to you. And why do you look at the speck in your brother's eye but do not consider the plank in your own eye. Hypocrite! First remove the plank from your own eye and then you shall see clearly to remove the speck from your brother's eye.[26].

Which one of us lives without moral flaws with which we wrestle? Who is totally free from having a plank in the eye which blinds until it is removed with God's help? Can we say we have reached such a level of maturity in our lives that there is nothing displeasing to God in us? Can we judge as God would judge? If not, perhaps we should deal with those areas in us that displease God and leave judgment of others also to God. The speck in your brother's eye should be left to God who can see your brother's heart and judge accordingly. I believe it is time we learn to love with God's love, preach the gospel, and leave the results to God.

Chapter 4

"INTO THE CLOSET THE HISTORY OF HOW GAYS GOT PUT INTO THE CLOSET AND WHAT THEY CAN DO ABOUT IT"

As I was doing this research, I found people who believed differently from the established church and were trying to do something about it. With their support, I found liberation and freedom. It also led me to search where all this anti-homosexual teaching had come from. I learned something that totally amazed me. For almost the first four hundred years of church history, there was no problem with homosexuality in the church. People of the same sex, known as natural eunuchs, were welcomed as members and held important positions in the church, including as advisors to bishops. This was like a light bulb going on in my head. It meant that the early church would have had no issue with my being gay. They would even have allowed me to hold office in the church. So why did the church change to its current anti-homosexual teachings? How did this position become the predominant view of the majority of the Christian world? If the Bible does not teach against homosexuality, then where did this teaching originate and why?

As I studied further, I found out that the decision to condemn homosexuality was, in part, politically-motivated. It derived from a power struggle within the church over the orthodox church doctrine interpreting the nature of Jesus the Christ. A lot of those that we today label homosexuals were Arian in their theology. They defined Jesus as a created being inferior to God the Father. Also, some Arians maintained that God was not the Father of Jesus in a procreative sense. Instead, they said that God adopted Jesus as His Son through grace. That view was ultimately condemned by the church in favor of the doctrine of the Trinity, which maintained that Jesus and the Father were coequal and have always existed. The western Roman Catholics upheld the Trinitarian position. Having won, the victorious orthodox bishops decided to punish the homosexuals for supporting the wrong belief. The punishment brought the first pronouncements against homosexuality. They also led a re-interpretation of what the Bible taught about homosexuality. From then on, the teaching of the Catholic Church would be that homosexuality was morally wrong. Orthodox Christian leaders taught that the Bible unequivocally condemned homosexuality. Anyone who was a practicing homosexual was of the devil; therefore, they could not possibly be Christian unless they were delivered from homosexuality. Thus the closet was born. Homosexuals were told to abstain from all sexual activity otherwise God would condemn them. They quickly learned to remain hidden in the closet. If they came out, they risked being excommunicated from the church and ruined by being publicly exposed as a homosexual. They could also have been put to death or castrated. In my research, I discovered that on May 14, 390 there was an imperial decree issued. [27].

It was posted at the Roman hall of Minerva, which was a gathering place for artists, writers and actors. [28].

The decree criminalized the sexual practices of those whom we call homosexual men. This had never happened previously in the history of Roman law. Prior to 390, only one form of homosexuality was identified. It was a man or youth who could exhibit attraction towards women but chose not to. Instead they agreed to, or were forced to, play a female role in intercourse with other men. They were called eunuchs. They were not defined by the incompleteness of their physical anatomy, but by their sexual orientation. Since natural eunuchs were men lacking a desire for women, like today's homosexual men, they would not have been covered by the sex laws as the laws only applied to males. Eunuchs would not have been deemed to be male. Instead, maleness would have required the man to play the role of penetrator and procreator. Men had to be able to produce children. If they could not, or would not, then they failed the ancient criteria for being called male. Masculinity in the ancient world was not defined in contrast to women, but to homosexual men. By this definition, only heterosexual men would have been considered male, since potency with women was the primary proof of masculinity. [29].

Exclusively homosexual men were often called nonmale—neither male nor female, androgynous, or third sex—but never male. Sex between eunuchs and males was prohibited; however, sex between eunuchs was not. [30].

Eunuchs included a category of men in the ancient Mediterranean world who were called "natural" or "constitutional" eunuchs. [31].

They were defined as having no physical defects except for a "peculiar mental state". [32].

They were what we would call today "born homosexuals". The law made a difference between them and castrated men, and also between homosexuals and those with physical defects. Natural eunuchs could marry if they wanted, and bequeath property, and adopt. [33].

Castrated men, or those with physical defects, could do none of those things. In the ancient world, starting with Babylon and on through the late Roman Empire, eunuchs served two major roles in ancient society. They served as priests in pagan temples, and as domestic servants in wealthy households and royal palaces. They had a tradition of spirituality and of being close to power. This made them of great help to the bishops that they supported and a threat to those they opposed. [34].

This put them on a collision course with Roman Catholic authorities opposed to their Arian views and who wanted the power the eunuchs exerted for themselves. Thus began the identification of homosexuals as powerful enemies of the church and of Catholic doctrine. This is not the place to discuss the merits of whether they were right or wrong it is simply to acknowledge that it happened. A third position eunuchs had in ancient society was a traditional role as sexual passives. Because they were not "male", this practice was legal in both pagan and Biblical law throughout all previous history. The Christian emperor Constantius II issued a decree implicitly recognizing eunuch marriages as long as they didn't involve a "male" in a passive role. Constantius was also known to be devoted to his eunuchs, courtiers and wives.[35].

As stated above, the definition of a eunuch began to change in the fourth century. In the third century, Clement of Alexandria had defined the eunuch as one who was not unable to have sex but as one who was unwilling to have sex. [36].

Then, in the fourth century, Epiphanius of Salamis said that eunuchs were incapable of doing anything sexually because they allegedly lacked the "divinely created organs of generation". [37].

This was the first time that eunuchs were defined on the basis of their physical anatomy rather than their sexual orientation. By adopting that view, the church successfully reduced natural eunuchs to a physical defect. They then used that as an excuse to deprive them of their religious credibility. Against this backdrop the Arian controversy raged, prompting the campaign against homosexuals. The Roman Catholic Church was looking to debase their powerful enemies and so moved to outlaw the sexual life of homosexuals. In 389, neo-Arian eunuchs were denied the right to make or benefit from wills. [38].

This was technically done as a means of combating heresy. Meanwhile, the emperor Theodosius had earlier committed an atrocity against the residents of Thessalonica. He was excommunicated from the church by the Bishop of Milan, St. Ambrose. Theodosius then crawled to Ambrose begging for forgiveness and reinstatement. Ambrose relented and promised to restore the emperor after an eight-month penance. On May 14, 390, a month after that meeting, Theodosius issued the decree condemning homosexuality. Laws were quickly changed to reflect this new definition based on physical anatomy and the death penalty of burning in fire was established. The decree was allegedly issued as a means to combat heresy. It promptly removed many Arians from positions of authority and gave them to Roman Catholics who supported the church and the Trinitarian position. This greatly increased Roman Catholic power, especially over doctrine.

Once having established power over imperial legislation, especially in regards to religion, Catholic authorities would never look back. They had gotten rid of heresies and stripped the eunuchs of their religious credibility. That being the case, there was no one left to challenge them so they started to re-interpret the scriptures. They began to teach that Jesus, when talking about eunuchs, was referring to men suffering from physical defects. They also began to teach that those engaging in homosexual acts were guilty of the sin of Sodom. All who could have challenged the new teachings were either gone, discredited, or in the closet hiding.

In the seventh century, with the passage of the Visgothic Code, it was ordered that every man found to be guilty of a homosexual act should be castrated. By then, merely having an intact penis and testicles were enough to make you a male, not sexual orientation as previously.

My research showed that for almost the first four hundred years of church history it was okay to be homosexual and to hold office in the church. The decision to outlaw homosexuality was in part a political decision to increase the power of the Roman Catholic Church. Since 390, the teaching against homosexuality has been passed down as authoritative leading almost all of Christianity to accept it as truth, and the proper understanding of the scriptures. The research has shown that there is a better interpretation and understanding of the Bible on the subject of homosexuality. This departs from the traditional politically-motivated teaching and it represents a more accurate picture of what the early church thought.

It is time to present the facts as they truly exist. It is time to restore gays, lesbians, and trans-gender people to full rights in the church; rights they enjoyed for the first four hundred years of church history. The church is long overdue in righting the wrong committed against homosexuals in 390. It is time to teach what the Bible actually says, and what the apostles actually taught. We need to be brave enough to let go of the prejudices and bigotry that try to destroy homosexual people. Instead it is time to destroy the closet forever so that no gay person ever has to hide again. We need to make sure that our churches our inclusive, inviting all even as Jesus did. That is the vision we need. One church united, regardless of race, sex, or sexual orientation, ready to witness to our world for the cause of Christ.

It should be noted here that the ancient church practiced same-sex marriages and even had a rite for it. In doing some research on the subject, I came across an article entitled "When Marriage Between Gays Was a Rite". It was written by Jim Duffy of Dublin, Ireland, and published in the Irish Times on August 11, 1998. He writes in his article that there was evidence of the Roman Catholic Church allowing and performing same-sex marriages well into the 18th century. He believes that the Christian attitude towards same-sex marriages has changed over the years. In Kiev, Russia, an art museum contains a curious icon from St. Catherine's Monastery on Mt. Sinai. The icon shows two robed Christian saints, men dressed in wedding garments, with a Roman pronubus (best man) between them who happens to be Christ. The icon depicts St. Serge and St. Bacchus, two Roman soldiers who became Christian and were martyred. They are described by early Christian writers as having been joined together in life and St. Serge is described as "a sweet companion and lover of St. Bacchus". This confirms what the icon implied, that they were a homosexual couple. Their pronubus is pictured as Christ himself suggesting that Christ would have blessed the union rather than condemn it.

Evidence also exists that shows that there was an "Office of Same Sex Union" also known as "Order for Uniting Two Men" in the Roman Catholic Church up through at least the18th century. These ceremonies had all the trappings and symbols of a marriage ceremony for heterosexual couples. The community would gather in a church, a blessing of the couple before the altar would take place, their right hands would be joined, a priest would participate and serve the Eucharist to the couple, and there would be a wedding banquet afterwards. These unions were popular in Ireland in the 12th and 13th centuries, as well as in pre-modern Europe. The following is a litany taken from a Greek liturgical document called "Order for Solemnisation of Same Sex Union" used in the 13th century. The service began with invoking the names of St. Serge and St. Bacchus. It then called on God to "vouchsafe unto these Thy servants (N and N) grace to love another and to abide unhated, and not cause of scandal all the days of their lives, with the help of the Holy Mother of God and all Thy saints." The ceremony concluded by having them kiss the Holy Gospel and each other after which they are considered to be married. In a fourteenth century Serbian Slavonic "Office of the Same Sex Union" for the uniting of two men or women, it details the following. The couple were to lay their right hands on the Gospel while having a cross placed in their left hands. After kissing the Gospel, the couple were then required to kiss each other, after which the priest having raised up the Eucharist would give them both communion. These ceremonies were found included in a in a Greek prayer book of the sixteen hundreds. Homosexuality was technically illegal from late Roman times. Yet same-sex marriages continued to take place, even after anti-homosexual feelings began to sweep across Western Europe in the fourteenth century. At St. John Lateran in Rome (traditionally the Pope's parish church) it is recorded that in 1578 as many as 13 couples were joined together with the apparent cooperation of the local priests. They took communion together using the same nuptial scriptures as would be used in a regular wedding ceremony of a man and a woman, after which they slept and ate together. There is also a record of a woman to woman union in Dalmatia (modern day Turkey) in the eighteenth century.

This research poses some fundamental questions for modern day church leaders and heterosexual Christians. Given what has been shown to be fact concerning same-sex unions in the early church, what should be our attitude today? We have seen that the church has changed its views on homosexuality over the years, in part due to power politics. For the church to ignore the evidence would be a major evasion. The historical record shows that, for a good portion of the last two millennia, some churches throughout Christendom had no problem with homosexuality. Instead they accepted it as a valid expression of a God-given ability to love and commit to another person. It was seen as something to be celebrated, honored, and blessed. It is time for the modern church to adopt the same attitude of the early Church.

At this point, it might be helpful to correct a few misconceptions about gay people. Hopefully this will help non-gay people understand gays and what they are about. Many would say that they are willing to let homosexuals live as they want to. They are just opposed to us trying to force our lifestyle on others or trying to seduce young people into the homosexual lifestyle. These ideas are false. First, is it really true that some were forced or misled to become homosexual? Either they are or they are not. For most of us it is not a choice, but the way that God made us. The only choice for a homosexual is whether to accept their homosexuality or not. They can try living in the closet of fear, repression, frustration, and condemnation if they want. They can try to deny their homosexuality and live as society and the church says they should as heterosexual people. Experience has shown that trying to live like that leads to a lot of needless guilt, frustration, and condemnation. The other choice is to live openly as a gay person, free to be all they can be. They can choose to trust a God who loves them, people who accept and affirm them, living without guilt and condemnation. They can choose to let the closet be destroyed forever for them and never to return to it again. That is the choice I hope every gay person will make. The second misconception is that homosexuality is synonymous with being a pedophile. The majority of homosexual people would be as revolted with the thought of having sex with a child as the majority of heterosexual people would be. Research has shown no connection between homosexuality and child molestation. Thirdly, the term "homosexual lifestyle" is said to be code for promiscuity. There may be promiscuity in the gay community but is it at a higher rate than in the heterosexual community? If promiscuity cannot be used to deny the life of heterosexuality then it cannot be used to condemn homosexuality. Gay people do not want special treatment. They want the same rights, responsibilities and opportunities that are enjoyed by heterosexuals. They want equal treatment in the work place. They want to live openly as gay people without fear of being beaten or murdered for who they are. They want the same right to build families and relationships, and the right to love as accorded to everyone else. They want to be able to visit their loved ones in the hospital, and to make decisions affecting their loved ones, especially if they are dying. They want to be able to inherit property left by their partner, and receive the same benefits afforded to all married couples and to heterosexual couples who are just living together. Gays want to pursue the "American Dream" to become all we can be, which is no different than millions of other Americans.

As for the idea that we are trying to force our lifestyle or "agenda" on others, says who? The only "agenda" is to obtain the above rights that are guaranteed us by the United States Constitution. I know of no attempt by gay people to force their "lifestyle" on anyone. Indeed, it is the "Christian Right" and their evangelical allies who seem determined to force their lifestyle on every single gay American. They are signing petitions and placing anti-gay rights initiatives on the ballot. In trying to take away our rights, they have forced the gay community to rise up and fight. We wish to be treated as full citizens. We want to be recognized as human beings with the same needs, desires, and dreams as every other human being.

As for gay marriage, civil unions, or domestic partnerships, all we are asking for is the same right to express our love and commitment to our partners as heterosexual couples do in marriage. We want the same rights and benefits they have. In other words, end the discrimination against gay people. Blow the closet back to hell where it belongs. Let us enjoy what everyone else gets to enjoy. Some may fear that same-sex marriage would destroy traditional marriage. Why should it? Those who want to marry someone of the opposite sex will still be free to do so. Homosexual couples would be able to have the blessing of marriage and be able to openly commit to their partners like heterosexual couples. They would be able to enjoy all the benefits and responsibilities under law that comes with being married. Gay people are as devoted, patriotic and love their country as much as anyone else. They vote, serve in the legislatures of their state and country, serve in the military and believe in making freedom and democracy work for all.

As for the church, gays seek to be able to love God and serve Him with the rest of the Christian community, to be able to participate in all aspects of church life including the ministry if God calls us. We want to be accepted on the same basis as any other Christian including the right to all the sacraments of the church. Gays want our persecution ended and a new era of understanding and openness to exist between the church and the gay community. We don't want to be condemned. We do want to be accepted as brothers and sisters in Christ. We want the church to become an all inclusive body following the example of Jesus Christ, loving all as Jesus Himself did.

As we destroy the closet we allow gays to contribute to society, do what they can do and to realize their Godgiven potential. It is time to end the bigotry and discrimination based on sexual orientation, religion, gender, or anything else. Instead, we should be opening the "American Dream" to all people including gays, lesbians and trans-gender people. Let us all be proud of who we are. Proud of our heritage, our country, our religion or lack thereof, our freedoms, and the chance to be whatever we want to be. If gays are willing to invest the time, effort and determination to become something then let them do it. That is the America I believe our nation's founders fought to establish. It was to be a nation free from tyranny, and from domination by one person, group or religion. That was why the Bill of Rights was added to our constitution ensuring that our rights would be protected forever. That is the America in which most gays believe and serve. That is what we want for ourselves as well as for everyone else. We invite you to join us in this struggle to bring equality, liberty, and justice to all without exception.

We insist that acceptance and inclusion become the norm for all gay, lesbian, bisexual, and trans-gender people. We should be allowed to be ourselves as you are allowed to be you. If that is the America you want then come and join us and welcome aboard.

In recent days we have seen the ban on gays in the military done away with. The Supreme Court has struck down the Defense of Marriage Act, thereby ending marriage discrimination for gays at the federal level. We have also seen many states allow same-sex marriage.

We thank God for those beginnings and thank those who helped bring them to pass. However the fight has only just begun. We need to take our battle to the states until all 50 states recognize same-sex marriage. Then we need to continue our fight for the rights of our gay brothers and sisters until every nation on earth accepts them and all bigotry and bias has ended.

Chapter 5

WAS AMERICA FOUNDED AS A

CHRISTIAN NATION?

In recent years, there has been a call to return to our "Christian heritage". Many of the Christian Right-wing religious-political philosophy and their evangelical allies insist that our nation was founded as a Christian nation. They say that our government was established for the promulgation of the Christian faith. They insist that our government and laws were founded upon the Bible. They make the claim that our founding fathers were devout men of faith in God and the Lord Jesus Christ. According to them, our founding fathers intended to establish a government based on their "Christian" beliefs.

Is that really true? Were our founding fathers devout evangelical Christians or just nominal Christians?

Would their views have departed radically from what would be considered Orthodox Christianity? Would they have cared about sexual preference or orientation and what loving acts people do behind closed doors?

Are evangelicals right to condemn gays because of what they think our founding fathers might have done or thought?

The Christian religion was an important factor in the settlement of America. Five colonies, Massachusetts, Connecticut, Rhode Island, Maryland and Pennsylvania, were founded as religious communities. Almost all colonies had state-supported churches; however, they differed widely in their views of Christianity. In Massachusetts, the Puritans built the early colony on their ideal of a "Christian community." Some, such as Anne Hutchinson, who dissented from their theological standards, were banished. Religious intolerance enjoyed authority and power in the colony. Being different could mean banishment or death for those convicted of witchcraft in 1692. In the Massachusetts Bay colony, a dream could lead to your execution. If someone had a dream of you trying to bewitch them or in which they allegedly saw you consorting with the devil or demons, it could be enough to get you hanged. If you talked with or associated with accused witches, you could be executed.

Is that the type of America we want to go back to? Is this the "City on a Hill" that evangelicals and the Christian Right want us to emulate? By the time of the American Revolution, strict orthodox Christianity had been rejected by George Washington, Thomas Jefferson, Thomas Paine, Benjamin Franklin, John and Samuel Adams, Ethan Allen, James Madison, and many others of our founding fathers in favor of Deism. They believed in a God that created the world like a clock-maker creates a clock and lets it unwind over the course of time. This image of God no longer intervened in human affairs. They believed that only that which could be understood with the mind's logic and reason was true. Consequently they rejected the deity of Christ, His virgin birth, His performance of miracles, and His resurrection and ascension into heaven. To them, such ideas were illogical and unreasonable.

Thomas Jefferson, who was the principle author of the Declaration of Independence and third president of the United States, rewrote the Bible during his second term in office. It has become known as the Jefferson Bible. In it, he eliminated all the Old Testament, and all the miracles of Christ. He chose to concentrate instead on the moral and ethical teachings of Christ as he saw them.

Here are some statements taken from some of our founding fathers which show what they actually believed:

"Have you considered that system of holy lies and pious frauds that has raged and triumphed for 1500 years" (John Adams in a letter to John Taylor in 1814, quoted by Norman Cousins in 'In God We Trust': The Religious Beliefs and Ideas of the American Founding Fathers (New York: Harper and Brothers 1958. p. 106-107)

"The question before the human race is, whether the God of nature shall govern the world by His own laws, or whether priests and kings shall rule it by fictitious miracles." (John Adams in a letter to Thomas Jefferson, June 20, 1815)

"I do not find in orthodox Christianity one redeeming feature. Religions are all alike—founded upon fables and mythologies. Millions of innocent men, women, and children, since the introduction of Christianity, have been burned, tortured, fined and imprisoned, yet we have not advanced one inch to uniformity. What has been the effect of this coercion? To make one half of the world fools and the other half hypocrites." (Thomas Jefferson, Notes on the State of Virginia, 1781-1782)

"The day will come when the mystical generation of Jesus, by the Supreme Being as His father, in the womb of a virgin will be classed with the fable of the generation of Minerva in the brain of Jupiter." (Thomas Jefferson in a letter to John Adams, April 11, 1823)

"An amendment was proposed by inserting the words, 'Jesus Christ . . . the holy author of our religion' which was rejected. By a great majority in proof that they meant to comprehend, within the mantle of its protection, the Jews and the Gentile, 50 the Christian and the Mohammedan, the Hindoo and the Infidel of every denomination." (Thomas Jefferson, The Autobiography of Thomas Jefferson, 1743-1790, 1821)

"During almost fifteen centuries has the legal establishment of Christianity been on trial. What has been its fruits? More or less, in all places, pride and insolence in the clergy, ignorance and servility in the laity; in both, superstition, bigotry, and persecution.

In no instance have the churches been guardians of the liberties of the people. Religious bondage shackles and debilitates the mind and unfits it for every noble enterprise." (James Madison, A Memorial and Remonstrance, 1785)

"The way to see by faith is to shut the eye of reason. Lighthouses are more helpful than churches." Benjamin Franklin, Poor Richard's Almanack, 1758) Franklin in his autobiography said that, although the Rev. Mr. Whitefield had prayed for his conversion, he never had the satisfaction of believing those prayers were ever heard.

In reference to George Washington a good friend of his, Dr.Abercrombie, when asked said, "Sir, Washington was a deist."

The above statements show what our founding fathers actually believed. They were not orthodox in their beliefs. In most references to God, having to do with the establishment of our country, it is this deistic God that is being referred to. This was a God who is the Creator, the Supreme Being, and Judge of the world, the God of nature,but not necessarily the personal living God of the Bible. The living God, abiding in us and walking with and helping us would have been foreign to them.

Some might point to the fact that when our country was founded nearly every state had state supported churches. Their ministers were paid by the state. This they would say is proof that we were intended to be a "Christian" nation. Not true, however. Many founding fathers opposed state-supported churches. They were in the forefront of the battle for the separation of church and state in favor of religious freedom for all.

There were major problems with state-supported churches that led to their disenfranchisement in all states by 1830. In states with state-supported churches, a society was created in which religious differences resulted in ostracism. Religious dissenters could be asked to leave and if they came back, they could be executed. Ministers were paid by the government. Everyone had to pay taxes to the state-supported church. It didn't matter if you were a member of that church, believed in its teachings, or wanted anything to do with it. You could have preferred to be left alone to practice your own religion or none, if you chose. That wouldn't have mattered.

By the fact you were a resident of that state, you had to pay taxes automatically to the state-supported church. Since ministers were paid by the state, they were beholden to the state and not to their congregations.

This meant that congregations were often ignored by their "ministers" or were shepherded by hirelings whom the state-appointed ministers brought in. The wealthy sat on the benches in the courts, and in the legislatures that decided who became ministers and where. This had the obvious effect of ministers needing to curry the legislatures favor so they could keep their jobs. The poor and others were often left on the sidelines while the wealthy and influential people controlled and ran the churches.

Is that the kind of America we want to go back to? A place where bigotry, intolerance, and injustice are practiced every day in the name of God and the Bible? Do we really want only one Christian tradition to tell us how to live our lives? If our answer is yes, then how will we choose between the myriad of sects and denominations of Christendom as to which one should be our national religion? Do we want to see an outbreak of religious wars such as ravaged Europe in the sixteen and seventeen hundreds? Wars where each sect tried to establish dominance over all other sects. Is that what we want? I pray that we have moved beyond all that. I trust we can see that it is in our diversity that we have gained strength. We have been made strong as we have absorbed and learned from each of the various cultures that have come here to be a part of our great country. I pray that we can each learn from the mistakes of the past. Where possible, we need to seek the forgiveness of those we have offended, and of God. We need to find the moral courage and strength to do what is right because that is what our consciences and beliefs tell us. It is time for reconciliation to begin between all races, genders, and sexual orientations.

What kind of government did our founding fathers establish and pass down to us? Was it a "Christian" government that would promote "Christian" morality? Let's take a look at the Preamble to the United States Constitution and find the reasons why our founding fathers established the government they did.

"We the people of the United States, in order to form a more perfect union, establish justice, insure domestic tranquility, provide for the common defense, promote the general welfare, and secure the blessings of liberty, to ourselves, and our posterity, do ordain and establish this Constitution for the United States of America."

Six reasons are given here for the establishment of our government:

1. To form a more perfect union
2. Establish justice
3. Insure domestic tranquility
4. Provide for the common defense
5. Promote the general welfare
6. Secure the blessings of liberty

Take note that nothing is said about promoting a religion or a moral code. As a matter of fact, the first amendment to the Constitution expressed our founding fathers' views on religion quite nicely.

"Congress shall make no law respecting an establishment of religion, or prohibiting the free exercise thereof . . ."

Our founding fathers intended for government to be neutral to religion, neither supporting nor opposing any religion. Their view was simple. No religion was to be given preference over another.

Neither was there to be a religious litmus test for those running for political office. All religions were to have an equal opportunity to flourish, grow, seek converts, and proselytize. They were also able to raise money, publish religious tracts and materials, and ordain their own ministers, free from any government interference.

People were to be free to practice whatever religion they wanted or none at all if that is what they preferred. Religion was seen as good as it kept the peace and tranquility of a community from being disturbed.

Religious people made good citizens, obeyed the laws, voted, and lived quiet lives. They weren't out fomenting rebellions and revolutions, and they did well to their neighbors. They also worked within the system to bring about change. At the same time, religion was seen as bad, keeping people in bondage and superstition and keeping them from being free to think for themselves. It was seen as stirring the people up as each sect tried to prove that they represented the true church and tried to convert everyone to their beliefs.

Our founders were familiar with the religious wars in Europe and the persecution of non-Anglicans in England. These had resulted in many of their forefathers immigrating to America. Those wars and persecutions were the last thing our founding fathers wanted to have happen here. By making government neutral, all people would be free to practice the religion of their choice. They would also be free to practice none if that suited them better.

Some may ask: How does this political history apply to our study on homosexuality? It shows that the founding fathers did not establish a "Christian" nation. Neither did they establish an explicit moral code beyond public law that all Americans would live by. At the time of the founding of our nation, there were sects that prohibited their members from engaging in sex at all, even between husband and wife. There were also sects who were into free love and wife-swapping. All operated without any interference from the government. The Christian Right and their evangelical allies are wrong when they say that the United States was founded as a "Christian" country. They are equally wrong when they say that the Bible was to be the standard by which all Americans were to be judged along with our laws. The only laws that might be found on sex would have been those passed by a local community. Prostitution flourished openly as did saloons, especially in the West. The Christian Right cannot point back to our supposed "Christian" heritage to condemn homosexuality.

That heritage is a fiction. Our founding fathers were Deists whose religion said nothing about sex. If the Christian Right wants to go back to the religion of our founding fathers then they should forget Christianity and opt for Deism.

It is time for the government to get back to doing what it was established for. Government needs to get out of the bedroom and private lives of people who are not causing public disorder. It is long overdue for government to once again go neutral on religion, neither supporting nor attacking it. The rights of the individual should be supreme, not those of the government. It is time we return to ". . . a government of the people, by the people, and for the people . . ." as Abraham Lincoln put it. The "Imperial Presidency" needs to be eradicated now and the government be made the servant of the people once more. The time has come to live up to the ideals that Thomas Jefferson penned in 1776.

"We hold these truths to be self-evident, that all men are created equal, that they are endowed by their Creator with certain unalienable rights, that among these are Life, Liberty and the pursuit of Happiness".

Our founders believed in an implicit, natural moral order that free people could understand and realize by the use of reason. Originally those truths were thought to apply only to free white men. Later those words were expanded to include, blacks, women, and the American Indian, as well as others. It is time to extend those same words to include all gay and lesbian Americans. It is time to allow us the same right to life, liberty, and the pursuit of happiness.

The time has come to teach tolerance. We need to recognize that it is through our diversity that we have received strength. Together we have worked to build our great nation. We have done this by sharing our heritage, ideas, hopes and dreams as we together have pursued the American Dream. The result is we have built a great nation that we need to protect and die for if necessary. Let us embrace that tradition that prizes an implicit natural (God-given) morality that reason recognizes and reasonable people seek to realize. We need not fear our diversity, but embrace it. Then let us keep doing that until all injustice, bigotry, racism, sexism, and intolerance have been overcome by love and understanding.

Together let us seek the time when all war, murder, and strife between nations is overcome by God's peace. We need to keep doing it until we see the literal fulfillment of the angel's proclamation on that first Christmas night.

Then the angels proclaimed "Peace on earth and good will toward men." Will you join me and say, "Amen, let it be"?

Will it be easy? No. Will it happen overnight? Not likely; however, we need to strive to realize the ideal.

The eighteenth century British parliamentarian, Edmund Burke, said, "When bad men combine, the good must associate; else they will fall one by one, an unpitied sacrifice in a contemptible struggle." We must gather together as gay and lesbian people if we wish to see our cause triumph. If we are divided or try to fight alone, we will fail. We cannot remain silent to injustice, bigotry, or hatred.

Neither can we remain silent any longer to the plight of our gay, lesbian, and transgender brothers and sisters. If we do, then we acquiesce to injustice and give our approval to it. We need to make our voices heard loud and clear, remaining silent no longer. We need to use every legal means to bring about change for the better.

United we can make a difference even as the blacks did in he late nineteen fifties and early sixties, resulting in the passage of the Civil Rights Act of 1964 and the Voting Rights Act of 1965. This gave the blacks new rights which had been denied them. Mahatma Gandhi, through uniting the people of India in a campaign of non-violence, won independence for his nation. Today we can do the same. Uniting, we can win equality and acceptance for all gay, lesbian and transgender people.

In the next chapter we will look at some constructive steps we can take to help get the ball rolling. What can we do to help bring about change for the better?

Chapter 6

A CHRISTIAN'S CALL TO ACTION
WHAT WE CAN DO NOW?

How can we make our voices heard? Where do we start towards moving forward to greater and better days?

The following is a list of four simple things we can do to begin to make our mark.

1. We need to start with ourselves

Examine yourselves as to whether you are in the faith. Test yourselves . . . [37].

The first thing we need to do is check ourselves. Do we truly embrace the truths that have been shared here?

Are we all inclusive in our attitude as Jesus was? If we are in the closet, are we ready to come out and destroy the closet forever? It is long overdue for all gay people to do so. The ones mentioned in the Bible as hiding are those who reject Christ. At His second coming they hide in caves praying for the mountains and rocks to fall on them.[38]. We are not of that class, but are those who have chosen to follow Christ as gay Christians. Since we are being what God has made us to be, loving and serving

Him, we don't need to be hiding. Instead, we need to be letting His light and love shine through us to others.

Many organizations, hotlines, websites, and counselors stand ready to help. Many churches are open and affirming of gays in their midst. They work with all gay, lesbian, bisexual, and transgender people affirming them in their faith. They also accept their gifts and talents in their churches and even ordain them to the ministry.

If you are heterosexual, you need to make a quality decision that there is nothing wrong with homosexuality and gay people. Make it your irrevocable decision from which you will never retreat. You need to openly embrace the truths that have been shared in this book.

Be fully accepting of all gay, lesbian and transgender people as creations of God like yourself. Affirmation of all who are gay needs to become an everyday occurrence with you. Finding ways to fight discrimination, bigotry, and violence against the gay community, needs to be encouraged. Above all, you need to make a commitment to equality and justice for all, including gay people.

2. We Can Pray

I am a firm believer that prayer changes things. I am also an equally firm believer that God may not move until His people pray. Certain types of demonic power cannot be broken unless we pray. It is an active way to tear down the demonic enemy's strongholds and power. It is a way to see change in people, nations, events, and circumstances surrounding us and affecting our world today. Jesus tells us:

. . . I say to you, if you have faith as a mustard seed, you will say to this mountain "move from here to there" and it will move; and nothing shall be impossible for you. However that kind does not go out except by prayer and fasting. [39].

In context, Jesus is speaking to His disciples who had just unsuccessfully tried to cast a demon out. They wanted to know why they had failed. Jesus infers that they failed because they weren't praying and fasting.

This caused them to lack faith. Jesus implies that if they had been praying and fasting then they could have cast out the demons. This also affirms that certain types of demonic powers will not be broken unless we pray. If we want to see an end to racism, bigotry, injustice, war, and other demonically-inspired evils, then we need to pray. This is predicated upon an Old Testament verse where God says:

If my people who are called by My name will humble themselves, and pray and seek my face, and turn from their wicked ways, then I will hear from heaven. And will forgive their sin and heal their land. [40].

In this verse, God gives us something we need to do in order to see Him move. We need to turn from all wickedness. That would be turning from hate to love, from doing injustice to doing justly, from making war to making peace. It would be turning from discrimination and bigotry against oppressed people, to loving, affirming, and accepting them for who they are. Once having done that then God says we can pray and He will hear and heal our land.

Another aspect of prayer is that we get to speak the word of God over a situation. We invite His presence into it, and begin to speak into existence the kind of world we want to have. Again Jesus speaking says:

Have faith in God. For assuredly, I say to you, whoever says to this mountain, Be removed and be cast into the sea, and does not doubt in his heart, but believes that those things which he says will be done, he will have whatever he says.

Therefore I say to you whatever things you ask when you pray believe that you receive them and you will have them. And whenever you stand praying if you have anything against anyone, forgive him that your Father in heaven may also forgive your trespasses. But if you do not forgive, neither will your Father in heaven, forgive your trespasses.[41].

A couple of things need to be noted here. First, our lack of forgiveness stops God from moving. By holding on to any sin, grudge, resentment, or anything else not of Him, we can effectively block God's blessing. The situation will remain that way until we deal with it through confession of our sin of unforgiveness and our positive acts of forgiveness. Once we have done that then we unleash the power of God to move on behalf of the blessing we seek.

Second, we need to believe that God is listening when we pray. If He listens then He will hear and answer our prayer beyond any shadow of doubt. When we have taken the time to pray, align our will with God's ideas and ways, and act out our convictions, then we will see something happen. When we can hear His still, small voice, recognize it and act on it, change will come. When we can do that, we will effectively close the door to Satan's subversion. When evil can't enter our souls, he can't bother us. As that happens, the kingdom of God will continue to expand until it covers all the earth. Satan's kingdom will shrink until there is no place left for him on earth forever.

3. We Need To Teach and Share in Love

And the things that you heard from me among many witnesses, commit these to faithful men who will be able to teach others also. [42].

We need to share the truth with others and teach them what we have learned. This needs to be done in churches, synagogues, mosques, and schools. It should include legislatures, radio and television programs, newspapers, and magazines. We must talk to our neighbors, friends and family, our children, our relatives and anyone else with whom we can find opportunity to draw into conversation. This needs to be done in love, as they are willing and able to hear what we have to say and accept it. If people have been unkind, it does no good to respond with unkindness. It is not helpful to rant and rave, hurl insults or beat up those who don't agree with us. We need to love them and let our light shine before them.

Then, as they see the fruits of our spirits, they will begin to ask questions as their curiosity is spiked. Then we can share the truth with them.

This is, of course, predicated on prayer and knowing the mind of God on how, when, and where we should share or teach. Prayer led by the Holy Spirit guides us into whatever action we take. Prayer will help us to forgive those who have done us harm. Communion with God's love enables us to act out of pure love that God's Spirit pours in into our hearts. With prayer, God will use us. Without prayer, we need to ask God to make prayer and knowledge of Him a reality in our lives. When that happens we will be ready to be effective agents for God.

We do not need dead martyrs for our cause. There have already been too many of them.

What we need are living martyrs (the word "martyr" means "witness" in the Greek) who have died to their old prejudices, ideas and ways. Now they are prepared to live and walk in love towards all. They are prepared to walk in the full truth of the Bible, as they have come to understand it and what it says about gay people. We need them to be a shining example of the way of love and a call to return to what Jesus called us to two thousand years ago. Lest we forget, He said:

A new commandment I give to you, that you love one another; as I have loved you, that you also love one another. By this all will know that you are my disciples, if you have love for one another.[43].

That is our call. May we go forth and do it.

4.   We Need to Get Involved

He has shown you, O man, what is good; And what does the Lord require of you but to do justly, to love mercy and to walk humbly with your God? [44].

We need to decide we are not in a spectator sport where we can sit on the sidelines and cheer on those who are playing. Instead we need to stand up and be counted. Too long have we been silent and evil has triumphed.

Now is the time for our active participation in what is just, merciful and loving.We need to fight for equal rights and protection for gay people because it is the right thing to do. If we will truly listen to our hearts, our consciences, and the still, small voice of God, they will tell us what is right and what we need to do. We need to support organizations, churches, Pride parades and festivals that are working for change.They are also working to get out our message of tolerance and acceptance.

It is high time to refuse to ever live in the closet again.

It is time to move beyond the fear, and bigotry of past generations. We need to learn about and accept the advances that have been made in scientific knowledge about the origin and nature of homosexuality. That scientific knowledge needs to be incorporated into our understanding of the Bible and its interpretation for modern day society.

As for where to begin, there are many ways to help.

Each of us needs to find the one that works for us and do it.

We need to do that because we have a dream of an America that is not based on a person's sexual orientation but on their worth as a human being. We hope for an America where a person is known by what they can give to their church, their society, family, friends, and job and not by their orientation or gender identity. We dream of an America that fully accepts the fact we are all children of God without exception. We demand an America where life, liberty and the pursuit of happiness will be open to all. We dream of the day when the closet is gone forever; when gay people can live openly without fear of harassment, bodily harm, or being murdered because of who they are; the day when discrimination, bigotry and hatred no longer stalk our land.

Instead we will be one united people known only as American and not by any other distinction. If that is a dream you believe in, I invite you to join us in bringing it to pass.

We need to remember once again the words of Edmund Burke, "When bad men combine, the good must associate; else they will fall one by one, an unpitied sacrifice in a contemptible struggle".

We have done too little on this issue in the past, but we cannot afford to continue that now. Instead, it is time for all good people to stand and be counted. The time is here to begin the process that will bring the dream to pass. Let the words of Patrick Henry ring loud and clear "United we stand, divided we fall". As we unite we will be heard. We will prevail regardless of what or who opposes and tries to stop us. It is the day for a new dawning as we reach out our hands to each other in love and acceptance. The hour has arrived for us to live up to the words of the Pledge of Allegiance which says, ". . . one nation under God, indivisible, with liberty and justice for all."

We may have a ways to go, but the drums are beating and the marchers are moving forth. The call has gone forth and many will respond. Today is the day of victory for us! Will you come join us?

Chapter 7

FINISHING THE RACE 'TIL I SEE HIS FACE

But we all, with unveiled face, beholding as in a mirror the glory of the Lord, are being transformed into the same image from glory to glory, just as by the Spirit of the Lord. [45].

Through all this I have learned a very important lesson. It is "Be Me". All the years that I spent trying to be someone else got me nowhere. They did get me a whole lot of anger, frustration, and condemnation; none of which I needed. Nor was any of it from God.

When I decided to be me with all that entails, freedom came. Liberty was the result of accepting myself as God created me to be.

It was also when I found the loving God of the Bible, and people who were affirming and ready to love me as I am. Since my coming out, some have left and want nothing to do with me anymore. To them, and those who disagree with me, I pray God's richest blessing be upon them. Moreover I pray they will one day be able to receive the truth and embrace it. I pray that one day they will see me as a fellow brother in Christ. Meanwhile, I bear them no grudge or ill will. Others, though not necessarily agreeing with me, have chosen to remain my friends. To them I say, "Thank you." Some, who were initially opposed to my being gay and my understanding of scripture, have had the grace to listen and learn. They are beginning to change and we are good friends. There have been many more people who are Finishing the Race 'til I See His Face willing to unconditionally embrace and fully affirm me as I am.

When I came out, I did so with fear and trepidation. I was fearful that everything I held dear would disappear. I was extremely fearful that my days of ministry were over. I should have known God doesn't close doors without opening others.

Since coming out, I am as busy or busier now than before. There is life after the closet. I am working with a couple of different churches and church organizations. I am teaching, writing, and helping with retreats, and have become a part of a religious community. More things have opened up for me since coming out than I could ever have imagined before. The best thing about it all is that I get to live openly as what I am; a gay Christian man.

Today, I can thank God for all I have been through. It has made me what I am. I thought I had imperfections and faults that kept me from being what God wanted me to be and which displeased Him greatly. Now I know differently. They were stepping stones to where I am now. They were the character builders that molded me into the man I am today. I have no idea of what might have happened had they not been there. I do know that, because of them, I can live as a free, openly gay man now with integrity. Having gone through all that I have has taught to me be a more loving and compassionate man than I might otherwise have been. It has caused me to want to reach out to others to help bring them out of the closet to freedom. Have I arrived at all

God has for me?

No, but I am on the road. It is true that I am perhaps not fully where I should be, but thank God I am not where I used to be. I am making some progress. I fully intend to stay in the race until the day I see His face.

Then, with open arms, I expect Christ to embrace me and invite me into the city and the home He has prepared for me. I fully expect to hear Him say "Well done" and that will be the proudest day ever for me.

I am glad that I can say with Dr. King, "Free at last, free at last, thank God almighty we're free at last". As I have studied, researched, and sought God, I have been freed and liberated. I pray if you are gay then the same will be true for you also as you have read this book. I am glad that for me the closet is gone. I am glad that in heaven there will be no closet for gays to hide in anymore.

There will be no distinctions in heaven either. We won't be gay, or not gay. We won't be black, white or any other color. We will just be children of God, forever with Him. The train is moving along the paths of our journeys. We are being changed until the day we see Him, when we shall be like Him.

Let us not give up or lose hope. Saint Paul says we are in a race and we each should strive to finish that race victoriously. Let us together finish the race until that day we see Him face to face. Let us not frown but go for the crown. Let us cross the finish line. We can wail and fail or push through to the victory. Christ is calling all to freedom and liberty, and to be with Him eternally.

How will we answer that call?

If you wish to comment about this book, please contact the author at:
pastorjohnwbrown@yahoo.com

We're Your Sons and Your Daughters

We're your sons
And your daughters,
We're your brothers,
And your sisters,
We are members of your churches
And we love Jesus too.
We share the love of Jesus
To everyone far and wide
For we are gay and we are Christian

Who love Jesus just like you.
We're your neighbors, we're your family, we're your friends and we're
your buddies, we're your teammates, we're your room mates, and your
coworkers too,
We struggle to pay the mortage
And to see the bills paid too,
And we are gay and we are Christian who love Jesus just like you.

We are proud of who God made us,
We are proud that He has saved us,
We are proud that He has called us.
And we are proud to serve Him too,
We are proud that Christ receives us
And His arms are open wide
To all who will receive Him gay, straight, or otherwise.

We're your sons
And your daughters,
We're your brothers,
And your sisters,
We are members of your churches
And we love Jesus too.
We share the love of Jesus
To everyone far and wide
For we are gay and we are Christian
Who love Jesus just like you.

John W. Brown

End Notes

1. Genesis 19:4-5
2. Genesis 19:8
3. Genesis 19:14
4. Ezekiel 16:49-50
5. Isaiah 14:12-15
6. Proverbs 16:18
7. Leviticus 18:22
8. Leviticus 20:13
9. I John 3:23
10. Kathryn M. Ringrose, The Perfect Servant:Eunuchs and the Social Construction of Gender in Byzantium, University of Chicago Press: Chicago, 2004.
11. Matthew Kuefler, The Manly Eunuch: Masculinity, Gender Ambiguity and Christian Ideology in Late Antiquity, University of Chicago Press: Chicago, 2001.
12. Readers should check Mattai the Preacher's website homosexualeunuchsandthebible. com for his extensive word studies documenting his contention that born eunuchs/ gay men played a significant role in ancient cultures as well as within the Bible.
13. Matthew 19:12
14. Acts 8:26-39
15. Mark 16:15
16. Matthew 28:19
17. Romans 1:21
18. Romans 1:28
19. Romans 1:22-25
20. Romans 1:26-27
21. I Corinthians 6:9-10
22. J. Paul Sampley, "The First Letter of the Corinthians: Introduction, Commentary and Reflections" in The New Interpreter's Bible, volume x, Senior Editor, Leander E. Keck, Abingdon Press: Nashville, 2002 pp. 853-67.
23. 2 Peter 2:6
25. Jude 1:7
26. Revelation 21:8
27. Matthew 7:1-5

The following endnotes come from secondary sources and are not fully documented. They are presented for readers to make further research.

28. Mosaicarum et romanarum legum collatio, 5.3.1-2, edited and translated by Rev. M. Hyamson, London:1913 reprinted in Buffalo, 1997, pp. 82-83.
29. Columbia Encylopedia, 5th edition, New York, 1993, s.v. Minerva, p. 1782. s.v. Minerva, p. 1782
30. Wilhelm Ensslin, Die Religionspolitik des Kaisers Theodosius des Grossen, Munich, 1953 In: Sitzungsberichte der Bayerischen Akademie der Wissenschaften, Philosophisch-historische Klasse, Year 1953, No. 2
31. Institutes of Justinian 4.18.4.
32. Seneca, De ira 1.21; Juvenal 6.371-373, 10.306; Martial 6.2, 9.6.4, 9.8.5; Silvae 4.3.16; Suetonius, Nero 28, Domitian 7
33. Digest of Justinian 50.16.128
34. Ibid., 21.1.1.9 in conjunction with 21.1.5-6 and 21.1.38.7
35. Ibid. 1.7.2.1, 1.7.40.1, 23.3.39.1, 28.2.6
35. Athanasius, History of the Arians, 5.38
37. Sextus Aurelius Victor, Epitome of the Caesars, 42.19
38. Clement of Alexandria, The Educator, 3.4.26.
39. Epiphanius of Salamis, Basket of heresies, 4.3.2-5.
40. Code of Theodosius, 9.7.6
41. 2 Corinthians 13:5
42. Revelation 6:15-17
43. Matthew 17:20-21
44. 2 Chronicles 7:14
45. Mark 11:22-26
46. 2 Timothy 2:2
47. John 13:34-35
48. Micah 6:8
49. 2 Corinthians 3:18